The Vermont Ghost Guide

Joseph A. Citro

The Vermont Ghost Guide

Art by Stephen R. Bissette

University Press of New England

HANOVER AND LONDON

Published by University Press of New England,
One Court Street, Lebanon, NH 03766
www.upne.com

Text © 2000 by Joseph A. Citro
Illustrations © 2000 by Stephen R. Bissette

ISBN-13: 978-1-58465-009-6
ISBN-10: 1-58465-009-5

Printed in the United States of America   5   4

CIP data appear at the end of the book

Contents

Preface

Why Not a Ghost Guide?

We have guides to Vermont Birds, guides to Vermont Trees, guides to Wildflowers, even a guide to Vermont Cows—so why not a Vermont Ghost Guide?

Ghosts have been part of the Vermont landscape for hundreds of years, since long before Champlain sailed down the lake. And those early native American spirits are still with us, though they've been upstaged by specters of every ethnic persuasion, marking each phase of Vermont's historical development.

In earlier books I have speculated about the size of Vermont's ghost population and wondered who might be better represented on the census charts, the living or the dead.

Though I have never seen a ghost, I have spent years learning where they are. And on these pages my friend Steve Bissette will use his magic wand—an artist's pencil—to summon them.

We will visit all corners of the state and meet many of the vengeful vagrants, lovelorn ladies, and lonely lads who lurk in Vermont's eternal shadows.

This Guide is a first-ever effort. As far as I know, no one has ever tried to catalogue all of Vermont's haunts. However, as a true census of Vermont ghosts, *The Vermont Ghost Guide* can be little more than a beginning. After all, ghosts are elusive critters; I am convinced we missed a fair number.

Why? Because ghost-finding presents a number of predictable problems. For example, many Vermonters who are happily cohabiting with ghosts would just as soon not broadcast the fact. Though they are remarkably matter-of-fact about their invisible housemates ("Well, they don't eat much"), they would just as soon their private residences remain private.

Churches present a unique problem. As you might imagine, there are several haunted churches and religious buildings in Vermont. Unfortunately, their stewards choose to keep the details under strict lock and key. If I can't root out the specifics, I can't tell the story.

Perhaps the largest group of spirits who've eluded the *Ghost Guide* are the ones I simply haven't heard about yet. With your help they will come to light for subsequent editions. So here's your chance: Become a census taker. Look at the end of the book for the address.

Introduction

Why a Ghost Guide?

In South Burlington, about a mile down Dorset Street from the high school, there is an old two-story brick house on the left. Rumor attributes to it something of a supernatural rarity: a haunted porch. Apparently its resident ghost on the second floor doesn't like furniture. Chairs, tables—in fact, most anything left there at night—will get heaved over the balcony before morning.

Or at least that's the story.

If I question the speaker a little more, he's likely to say, "Well, I'm not sure it's on Dorset Street. Maybe it's Spear Street. I know it's somewhere around the high school . . ."

Such is often the nature of ghostly tales: Because they are *friend-of-a-friend* stories, they may lack precision of locale, detail, or simply recall. So the need for a ghost guide is evident.

There is a second category of tale in which the facts may be a little more explicit. In such *first-person* cases the teller is also the experiencer. He or she knows the details, because he or she has had a personal interaction with the supernatural.

And—I have to admit it—there is a third type where the teller *creates* the experience.

Together these three—legend, experience, and fabrication—along with their various subdivisions—

make up a state's body of ghostly tales, a state's "spirit," if you will.

But, you may ask, after the imprecision and the fabrication, can ghosts be *real*? I simply cannot say. Only the experiencers know for sure.

I know the tales are real; they have tenacity and power. They affect what we think and what we believe, though—at least for now—their ethereal protagonists continue to elude so-called "definitive scientific scrutiny."

With all that in mind, please let me introduce you to some of Vermont's most venerable haunts along with some of their lesser known neighbors. A few are generated by firsthand experience. Some are folklore whose catalyst may be lost to memory. Only one— and I'm certain of this—is a fiction. I know because I made it up. Just one. I couldn't resist. And in so doing I leave you with the ghost-hunter's perpetual dilemma: to discern the fact from the fantasy.

So let the tour begin! Steve Bissette and I will be your guides to more than one hundred haunts from the Green Mountain State . . .

The Vermont Ghost Guide

A Gazetteer of Vermont's Haunts
Presented Alphabetically by Location

A Family Cursed

In 1823 the dying Merci Dale cursed the well-to-do Hayden family: They would die out in poverty in three generations. Strangely, they did. But are they also cursed to remain as ghosts in their brick Victorian mansion? What else would account for slamming doors, moving lights, and orchestral music playing in the empty former ballroom? But these phantoms are not alone. During prosperous times, William Hayden, Jr., was believed to have smuggled Chinese workers into the United States to work on the railroad he was building. When the illegal laborers died en route, they were buried in the fields behind the barns. Sometimes at night people still see the bobbing of lantern lights there, as if someone is forever digging graves . . .

sporting spirits

The sounds of people playing basketball can be heard day or night at Brigham Academy. Even when the gym is empty, people have watched a basketball dribbling across the floor—all by itself! A janitor once saw it bounce up against a wall and stay there. Locked doors open by themselves. Furniture rearranges itself. Cold air wafts from nowhere. A visiting psychic determined that the school was full of Native American spirits—but playful ones!

The Brady House

The two story Brady House, between the town hall and Route 108, was erected around 1830. Over the years a variety of ghostly activity has gone on within its brick walls. Invisible residents tromp across the attic, furniture moves around, and, on occasion, an elderly heavyset woman appears and vanishes. Strangest of all, piano music is sometimes heard. It must be a ghost playing a ghost piano, for no such instrument is in the house.

The 5-16 Ghost

Where routes 5 and 16 meet in the center of Barton is a historic building that was once the Barton Hotel. Supposedly a former manager was wrongly accused of theft and dismissed from his job. Disgraced, he headed west and vanished. But after death he returned to remind building occupants of the injustice that was done there. His ghostly footsteps can sometimes be heard in the building, followed by the unmistakable sound of an old-fashioned cash register opening and shutting.

Naked Natives

On an island in the Connecticut River at Bellows Falls, there is a group of factories. For years, out-of-place figures have been spotted outside and within the buildings, just across the canal from the post office. They are person-sized gray shadows that appear to be the naked, long-haired forms of American Indians. If seen inside a building, their legs are embedded in the floorboards as if walking on the ground beneath. Generally the apparitions are observed from behind, walking toward the water—as if moving toward the mysterious petroglyphs below Villas Bridge.

The Bottle Monument

Southern Vermont College, formerly bottle magnate Edward Everett's mansion, may be the most haunted house in Bennington. In addition to myriad mystical disturbances, phantoms are frequently seen. One of the most puzzling is the mysterious "Woman in White" who's sometime spotted within the house or prowling the grounds. A unique "pulsing ghost" was observed in a hallway, and the cartoon-like "dancing smoke" per-

formed on the theater stage. Outside, during broad daylight, students have witnessed mysterious "three-dimensional shadows"—a child and an adult—on the shores of the Upper Pond.

Three Men and a Boat

The abandoned village of West Castleton was once full of Irish slate workers. For amusement, they'd row across Lake Bomoseen to a tavern on the eastern shore. One night three men took a rowboat and headed out. Next morning the boat was found floating empty on the water. Nothing more was ever heard of them. The three had vanished completely; no bodies were ever found. But folks in the area say that on nights when the moon is full, a mysterious rowboat can be seen moving on the lake. No figures are visible within; no oars disturb the water. All that can be discerned is a dark, empty boat moving noiselessly across West Castleton Bay.

The End at Last

In 1872, in a boarding house on Oak Street, the ghost of Charles Dickens dictated the ending of his *Mystery of Edwin Drood* to medium Thomas Power James. Dickens and James were quite satisfied with the collaboration, promising additional efforts. However, critics and scholars were a little less enthusiastic. As Conan Doyle said, "It reads . . . like Dickens gone flat."

The Bloody Tower

On the grounds of the Brattleboro Retreat (formerly the Vermont Asylum for the Insane) stands a medieval-looking tower. It was constructed in the late nineteenth century by hospital inmates in the belief that physical labor promoted healthy minds. But not in all cases. Enough patients used the tower for suicidal leaps that the hospital closed it up. Still, some claim to have seen the spirits of those tragic dead lurking in the proximity of the structure, completing its haunted appearance.

Club Dead

The Brattleboro Country Club on Dummerston Road has generated persistent rumors of a low-level haunting. Though no one has been able to determine who the sporting spirits might be, employees frequently report hearing unintelligible voices coming from above the dining room. Other mysterious sounds from the same area—including footsteps walking overhead—leave workers too frightened to remain alone at closing time.

The Ghost Shaft

A Bristol boy and his dog set off to explore the abandoned treasure-digging cavities known as Hell's Half Acre on South Mountain. They never came home. Next spring a passing woodsman found the dog's skeleton near the opening of the fifty-foot shaft into which the boy had fallen. Today, when the moon is right and the shadows are long, folks swear they hear . . . something. The wind, perhaps? Or faint cries for help? Or perhaps the unearthly wail of a heartbroken hound?

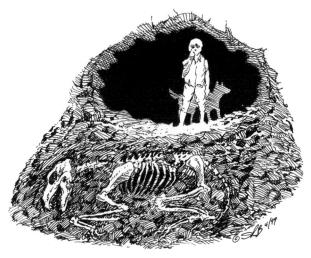

The Cursed Springs

A long-neglected geological anomaly—six healing springs flowing from a single knoll. Surprisingly, the mineral content of each is different. Indians were killed when Whites tried to seize the springs. A retaliatory curse was uttered by an Abenaki shaman, promising preternatural retribution if the waters were ever used for profit. Subsequently, at least four commercial spas burned mysteriously. Puzzled entrepreneurs gave up and abandoned the site. Wilderness reclaimed it. But at night, people say, you can still see the ghosts of the Indian protectors overlooking the springs or stalking silently across the surface of the water nearby.

Old Merchants Bank

The old brick building at 164 College Street used to house the bank's administrative offices. Employees would frequently enter a lunch room on the third floor and be surprised to see an old man sitting all by himself. He'd fade and vanish before their eyes. Many suspected it was the ghost of an attorney who'd once had an office there.

Vermont's Educated Spirits

The University of Vermont in Burlington is notable because it has at least fourteen haunted buildings. Low-level antics occur at the Admissions Building, Booth House, the Old Mill, Lambda Iota, and Wheeler House. The most venerable ghost is Henry, a suicidal medical student who haunts the gothic-looking Converse Hall. Though his story is tragic, his behavior is often playful. Phantoms have been seen at several buildings. There's a sad old lady in the Bitter-sweet and an irascible sea captain in the Counseling Center. And violent psychic upheaval has driven more than one after-hours toiler from the eerie halls of Grasse Mount.

Hospital Haunt

The maternity ward of the Fletcher Allen hospital is visited by a mysterious "presence." Labor and delivery nurses on evening or night shifts sometimes become aware that an unexplainable "something" is among them. Several reported being touched on the shoulder from behind. A patient having trouble with her shower rang for help. The ghost-nurse answered before the duty nurse could arrive. Apparently this caretaker spirit was formerly a combat nurse during the Second World War. She had seen so much sense-less injury and death that she devoted the rest of her life—and her afterlife—to birth instead. Though she passed away in the 1950s, she continues to report for work.

A Ghost's Tracks

Lakeside Avenue, which runs between Pine Street and Burlington Bay, crosses a railroad track. The Queen City Cotton Mill (later the G.E.) was located at that crossing. In the old days, before the underpass was built, the tracks could be dangerous for pedestri-ans. In June of 1900 a young factory girl named Marie Blais was struck and killed by a train there. Afterward, that stretch of track—and later the area between the track and the water—became Marie's "haunt." Hun-dreds of people saw and allegedly recognized her specter. Apparently there are no current sightings, but that doesn't mean Marie is gone. She's a ghost, af-ter all. Maybe she just chooses to remain invisible.

Two Stories

On North Street, across from the cemetery, there's a two-story house containing at least two ghost stories. The first floor was once a grocery store owned by a pious proprietor. Recently an unmarried couple was plagued by his moralistic spirit: Strange noises echoed through the rooms, the stove lit by itself, doors banged, footsteps stomped, and lights blinked. In 1992, to the couple's great relief, local ghost rescuers persuaded the godly ghost to move on. The second story, on the second floor, involves a woman who lived alone with her two dogs. Sometimes the ghost of a little girl stopped by to play with them; her other-worldly laughter could be heard from the kitchen. The dogs would chase an invisible ball, pick it up, and return it to the kitchen, where the ghost would laugh and throw it again. The perplexing process continued for up to an hour and may continue still.

A Ghostly Companion

In Cabot, an old road runs up and down the hill by an ancient graveyard. Although today there's not as much foot traffic as there once was, people still report an occasional chilly confrontation. Solitary walkers on that road at night will suddenly discover a stranger walking beside them. He might nod or salute in some quiet way. In more dramatic encounters he speaks, perhaps saying "Good evening," or asking one's name. Sometimes he introduces himself as "Mr. Anders." Then he'll be gone. Upon reflection, the startled pedestrian will realize the stranger had been dressed in an oddly old-fashioned style. Puzzled inquiry will reveal that a Mr. Anders had once been the hired hand at the house by the cemetery. But, when last seen, he had been many years in the grave.

Ghost Room

A yellow Queen Anne style house on the west side of town used to be a bed and breakfast. Of the unusual occurrences that have been reported there, perhaps the strangest involved a young woman who woke up at night to find her room had changed. She saw a door that had not been there during the day. The wallpaper, rugs, and linens were completely different. She tiptoed to the door, peeked out, and saw people in nineteenth-century clothing walking in the hall. One lady was carrying an old-fashioned oil lamp. The young woman suspected it was all an exceptionally vivid dream, though it didn't feel like a dream. She went back to bed and got in again. Then she saw the room "just shimmer" and return to twentieth-century correctness

Ghosts on the Fly

In the days when Castleton State College was the Castleton Medical Academy, grave robbing gave the place an unpleasant reputation. The medical school—now called the "Old Chapel"—inspired its share of ghosts. Sometimes they wander around campus, occasionally visiting the nearby Fine Arts Center. In addition to unexplained sounds and shadows, a ghostly young man is frequently spotted in the fly gallery of the theater. He just stands there watching. Then he disappears. The "Old Chapel" has its resident ghost. Though infrequently encountered, it is presumably a victim of old-time resurrectionists. Though the poor phantom is headless, its body is clearly that of a young woman. Supposedly her corpse was stolen by medical students and partially dissected. Relatives managed to recover most of the torso, but her head had been removed and hidden by the doctors-to-be. So far no one, including the phantom, has been able to find it.

Sam Connor's Other Self

Early in the nineteenth-century, Sam Connor was crossing a local swamp at night when he saw someone approaching him. As the other traveler got closer, Mr. Connor couldn't believe what he was seeing. It was his own double! Before vanishing, the look-alike spoke, predicting that Sam Connor would die within the year. All efforts to prevent the inevitable failed. Sam met his death in a construction accident one year later—to the day!

Disturbed Spirits

Not far from the general store in downtown Charlotte stands a house for years owned by psychologist Burt Zahler. It is apparently full of disturbed spirits. Centered in the room above the kitchen, the dark denizens occasionally let loose with a veritable storm of abnormal activity: pounding, three-dimensional shadows racing in and out of walls, doors opening and slamming. The psychologist had to call in a parapsycholgist to provide therapy for the unruly phantoms.

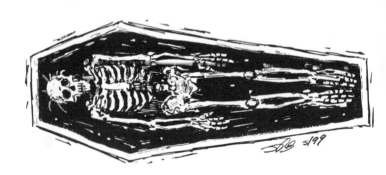

Inn Spirit

The grand, three-story inn at the center of town has a moody ghost who seems to hang out in Room 16. In addition to the usual noise-making, he frightens dogs, makes phantom phone calls, and scares housekeepers by appearing in the mirror. Occasionally he plays good-natured pranks like vanishing women's lingerie from Room 16, then materializing it elsewhere. But sometimes he'll pitch a fit. Once he hurled books from their shelves and smashed a statue of the Madonna.

The Ghost House

Just south of Milton, where Route 2 branches west from U.S. Route 7, is an area called Chimney Corner. The recent experience of a taxicab driver may explain why. As he was responding to a call in Milton he drove past the 2-7 intersection and saw a house engulfed in flames. He pulled over at a nearby store to phone the fire station. But when the trucks arrived there was no fire. And no house. Subsequent investigation revealed that the house had burned there fifty years before, leaving only the chimneys.

Vermont's Spirit Capital

In the 1870s, William and Horatio Eddy conducted elaborate materialization seances upstairs in their farmhouse. Dozens of costumed apparitions appeared every weeknight but Sunday. The specters were so vivid and stunning that people came from all over the world to witness them. Thanks to the Eddy brothers, Vermont became known as "The Spirit Capital of the Universe." The Eddys' mediumistic activities were frequently investigated, but never disproved. Today their house still stands, reincarnated as a ski club. And—according to many local tales—the ghosts still walk. Perhaps today William and Horatio have joined them.

Malletts Bay's Nuisance

In 1889 the Billings family lived on Thompson's Point Road. Not long after moving in, they began hearing sounds in the night. Gentle taps escalated to thunderous pounding. Walls shook. Invisible fingers whisked covers from the bed's terrified occupants. Sleep became impossible. Local spiritualists and a Catholic priest gave no relief. A *Burlington Free Press* reporter investigated but couldn't explain. Mr. Billings thought his family was being tormented by the spirit of a man with whom he'd quarreled in life.

Porters Point Road

There is a bit of troubled land on Porters Point Road where a Frenchman was hanged during the occupation. Apparently he had hated women, none more than his wife, whom he had murdered and mutilated. Though he was pursued and executed, his troubled soul lingers, affecting those who live in nearby houses. People don't stay long. Couples quickly fall into disharmony. Women leave or become unaccountably ill. Odd occurrences, sensations, and visions wreak havoc on this *mauvaise terre*.

The Mystery Woman

The West Dover Inn was built in 1846 by two brothers by the name of Bogle. Today, when weird events happen there, they're attributed to "Mr. Bogle." He makes things vanish and then reappear, messes with the electric lights, and bangs doors on windless days. It is harder to explain the female apparition that is sometimes witnessed. Does Mr. Bogle bring home company?

Inwood Oddities

The signs off the Old Silo Road still stand like ghostly guideposts leading you to the haunted spot. Though it is no longer open to customers, the Inwood Manor may have guests just the same. During its years as a bed and breakfast, remarkable phenomena occurred there: cold spots, doors opening and closing, lights flickering, vibrating tables, and a grand piano—covered and in a locked room—resounding through the halls. Phantoms were witnessed, including a disembodied hand, a woman in a striped dress, and an elderly man prowling the grounds outside. No one seems to know who the ghosts may be, but there have been many opportunities for spirits to take up residence. Over the years the building has served as a private home, a stagecoach stop, the dormitory for a croquet factory, and a bed and breakfast. Perhaps its ties to the spirit realm are especially strong: Several past owners were former monks.

Operatic Attic

The longest running player at the Enosburg Falls
Opera House has never been noted in a program. His
name is "Willy" and he has made himself known to
generations of performers. Willy is the ghost of a la-
borer who, while working alone in the attic, fell,
broke his leg, and lay alone and forgotten until he
died. Luckily, he is not vindictive. In fact, he is rather
mischievous, moving props and stealing playbooks.
While no one admits to having seen him, there are
numerous reports of "footsteps" in the attic. Many
adults refuse to work alone in the Opera House, especially with the doors closed.

The Maplewood Inn

So much ghostly activity has gone on here that one thinks there must be resident ghosts, as well as transients. The scent of cigars in this smoke free environment suggests rebellious spirits. Once they got downright violent and smashed the glass guard on a shower stall. But maybe the disruptive ones have left. A New Jersey woman watched a ghostly couple with a little girl walk out of the place. They were transparent and dressed in nineteenth-century style.

The Orb of the Valley

For a century or more, the so-called "Lost Nation" area near the East Fairfield-Bakersfield line has been haunted by a mysterious apparition. Called "The Orb of the Valley," it may be a Spook Light, a spirit, a UFO, or something totally unknown. Generally described as basketball sized, this red glowing sphere moves silently through the bushes, hovers eight or more feet off the ground, or soars off into the sky. It will occasionally approach people as if curious, but it never allows anyone to get too near. Many observers believe it displays a kind of intelligence.

The Ghost of Aunt Sally

After realizing Robert Fulton had ripped off his design for a steamboat, Capt. Samuel Morey grew dis-
couraged. In 1807 he sank his prototype, called the
Aunt Sally, somewhere in Lake Morey. He died soon
after. According to many, his ghost still walks. And
Aunt Sally still floats. Vermont's only ghost ship
sometimes rises from its watery grave and floats
soundlessly on the waters of Lake Morey, never cre-
ating a ripple.

The GHOST of "AUNT SALLY"   © 10/98

A Long Wait

Vermont's scenic Lake Morey Inn has its share of phantom guests. One of the most colorful is a flirtatious flapper who has been hanging around since the 1920s, when she passed away after overdosing at a New Year's party. She'd come there seeking a husband and apparently is still looking. Those who have seen her—usually attractive young men momentarily alone in one of the hallways—will suddenly become aware someone is standing beside them. They'll look to meet the wide eyes of a beautiful woman who'll then coyly vanish.

The Unruly Ghost

A small brick building, formerly a one-room school-house, still stands on Fisher Hill Road. After being converted to a private residence, various occupants have shared it with an occasionally visible someone who may once have been a teacher there. Flashes of lightning during nighttime thunderstorms reveal glimpses of the past: Chalkboards reappear on the walls and a transparent form sometimes materializes. The most striking manifestation is a shadow on the wall—a shadow of a ruler being tapped against the open palm of a silhouetted hand.

Turn Back the Clock

Over the years the grand white mansion near the end of West Shore Road has been used in many ways, from retirement home to private residence. Though corporeal occupants may come and go, its invisible population seems to be stable. At their most agitated they have been known to topple heavy pieces of furniture. At their most congenial, they'll drive up in phantom vehicles that can be heard but never seen. They'll laugh and chatter outside until someone tries to let them in. On at least one occasion, a whole room full of witnesses saw a plastic kitchen clock suddenly change direction as if the ghosts were trying to turn back the years.

A Railroad Disaster

On a subzero winter's night in 1887, the Montreal Express derailed and burned along with a high wooden trestle spanning the White River. Thirty-six people died in Vermont's worst railroad disaster. Today, the odor of burning wood lingers when a uniformed specter patrols the empty tracks at night. Faint cries and hopeless sobbing resound and a ghostly child appears at dusk. He wears old-fashioned clothing and hovers above the water, as if standing on a sheet of ice that long ago melted.

Sumner's Falls Phantoms

Before the Europeans came, Sumner's Falls was popular among Abenaki fisherman; it was perfect for catching salmon. Evidence of many Indian camps suggests it was a special place, one that was difficult to leave. Over the years people stopping at Sumner's Falls have witnessed dark moving shapes upon the waters. Sometimes they appear to be canoes filled with shadowy men. The apparitions never make noise as they paddle almost invisibly across the reflection of the moon on the dark water.

Host to Ghosts

Since it began life as a stagecoach stop in 1783, the Old Coach Inn has been host to ghosts. For some reason they seem to enjoy the closets of certain rooms. From these tiny enclosures, all sorts of commotion can occasionally be heard: the ruckus of parties, the rumor of conversation, even singing and piano music. Although such nocturnal nuisances may cost a few guests a good night's sleep, the ghostly antics are generally cheerful. The only identifiable spirit is the inn's long-dead builder, who returns and rocks almost invisibly in his favorite chair on the porch.

Riley's Ghost

The site of a former logging camp near Holland Pond is occasionally visited by what is presumed to be the ghost of Riley Caswell, once owner of the lumber company, who died in the 1880s. In life he was a vigilant sort, so those who have seen him in death figure he is just trying to keep an eye on things.

Black Ghosts

In the wooded area known as Lincoln Hill there is said to be a lost graveyard. Local lore maintains that it is the final resting place of a group of liberated slaves who for a time made their home in Huntington. The woods in this area, even during the day, have a creepy solemnity. For years, phantoms have been reported. They are said to be the spiritual remains of the many Black settlers whose lonely graves are lost among the dark trees and stony outcroppings.

The Thing in the Cellar

When young Anita and her mother moved into the house on Back Street, they knew nothing of its haunted history. One night Anita and her friend Mildred were left briefly alone. They heard heavy chains being dragged in what should have been an empty cellar. When they saw the trapdoor begin to open, the terrified girls raced to a neighbor's home. Today the house is long gone, and no one knows what manner of subterranean something was emerging from that hole in its floor.

Not Sheepish

In the late 1980s a carpenter working alone on the second floor of an old farmhouse on Route 114 (just outside Island Pond) chanced to look out the window. There he saw a pasture with a flock of sheep and a young girl herding them. Odd, he thought, there weren't any working farms nearby. But when he went out to talk to the girl, he couldn't find her. The sheep were gone, too, and the pasture was all grown up. Stubbornly, he continued working until he saw the girl again. This time she was waving to him. He quit the job and left.

Burned Up!

Until recently, a house stood on the Corner of Route 15 and Packard Road. Supposedly it was haunted by the ghost of an angry man. Starting in late 1985, the young couple living there experienced untraceable rattles and thumps. Things were moved around, doors opened and closed. A visitor stopped by one evening when the porch light was on. She saw an unfamiliar face glaring at her from the kitchen window. It frightened her away. She soon learned the house had been vacant and there was no electrical hookup on that porch. Later, another visitor was scared away when she saw footprints forming in the newfallen snow. Following many similarly odd occurrences, the house burned down. No one knows just why.

Private Room

Near the intersection of Route 2 and Cochran Road, an old schoolhouse, now a private residence, is said to be haunted by the spirit of "Bob Hand," a former owner. The building contains a special, sealed-off room to be used exclusively by the spirit. There are a table and chairs and other amenities intended to keep Bob occupied and out of the rest of the house. But—they say—he occasionally ventures out to explore.

The Simpson Farm

About 1910, Ed Simpson and his wife owned a farm on the line between Kirby and Lyndon. Ed was alleged to be a notorious drinker and wife beater. But he was a hard worker; he even plowed at night by lantern light. In time his wife became unable to tolerate his abuse. She took an ax to him during one of his drunken stupors, turning their bedroom into a charnel house. Subsequent owners have heard dragging, scuffing, and scraping, as if heavy furniture is being pushed across a wooden floor. Dark blood-like splotches that no paint can conceal appear on the walls and ceiling of the bedroom. And outside, people have seen lights in the fields, like lanterns bobbing up and down.

"Mad" Anthony's Ghost

The ghost of General "Mad" Anthony Wayne is most
often spotted at Fort Ticonderoga in New York. But
he may have a second home in Vermont. After his
1796 death, people started seeing his leather-clad
phantom walking the shores of Lake Memphrema-
gog. Sometimes, when the moon is right and the
shadows are long, the spectral general will pause,
turn, and face the water. Then, as if spotting something appealing on the far shore, he'll cross the lake—
by walking across the top of the water.

Scared Stiff

The building known locally as "the boarding house" was used in the nineteenth-century as a loggers' hotel and temporary residence for new settlers. Marriages and funerals were performed there. It was reincarnated as a ski club and later—after being purchased by a Long Island family—as "The Long Run Inn." They soon discovered they had a long-running if invisible guest in Room 6. Using odd noises and inexplicable shadows, the entity frightened family members and chased guests away. When the owner stayed alone in the room, she was shaken awake as her bed danced a little jig. Then she felt an arm around her. Paralyzed with fear, she said she finally understood the meaning of the term "scared stiff."

Native American Spirits

For years, people exploring the wilderness of the Green Mountain National Forest around Lincoln Gap have heard human-like calls or seen fleeting shapes moving among the twilit trees. Occasionally someone worries about the scent of a campfire, but can discover no flame nor smoke. On rarer occasions people spot what appear to be spectral Indians—one, maybe many—who subsequently dissolve or vanish. Some believe a whole colony of Native American spirits is in residence there. If so, they seem to be doing no harm. Quite the contrary: Most likely they are caretaker spirits doing all they can to keep the land healthy and undeveloped.

Nightmare On Depot Street

Just downhill from the Catholic Church stands a deceptively normal-looking two-story house. Rumor is that long ago a schoolgirl hanged herself upstairs. Yet something remains. Well-documented accounts tell of occupants being wakened by heavy furniture moving by itself. Family pets freely entered and left locked rooms. White ghost-like forms rose from the floor and vanished. A woman heard the shuffling slippered feet and wracking cough of her dead grandmother. And locked doors to the outside were found wide open, as if something had gone out. Or entered.

The Spirit's Spirits

The Cahoon House is the oldest Lyndon homestead. Its builder, Daniel Cahoon, was among the first settlers of the village. He had made his fortune in whiskey and never lost his taste for spirits. In 1811, perhaps under spirit influence, Daniel saved a local child from a charging bull and died in the process. But over the years he has continued as a member of the family and household, perhaps searching for the wine cellar his grieving wife had walled up in the basement.

Invisible Tears

The Riverside Day School, a neighbor of the Cahoon place, is said to house the ghost of a child who cries at night.

Beyond the Vail

Lyndon State College is located on the former Theodore N. Vail estate. Though Mr. Vail was the first president of the AT&T, it is his wife Emma who seems to have mastered communication—from beyond the grave. Most of her ghostly activities are in the theater, which stands on the site where she hanged herself. When a visiting comedian made jokes about her, his water glass fell off the table and rolled to the edge of the stage, where it righted itself. A magician had trouble with his equipment: Each time he set down his prop balls they'd spin away from him. A tightrope performer suffered the first fall of her career—she claimed to have been pushed. Sometimes an inexplicable "extra" appears during school plays. Regardless of the production, the "extra" is a woman, dressed in 1900s fashion.

Equinox

Vermont's grandest hotel is thought to be home to a number of ghosts, including that of Mary Todd Lincoln. Housekeepers avoid certain rooms where unaccountable noises, rapid changes in air temperature, voices, and vanishing objects puzzle those they don't terrify. Opening certain locked rooms exposes pyramids of piled chairs and peculiar paraphernalia. A security guard, upon entering especially haunted Room 329, witnessed lampshades spinning, rocking chairs rocking, and the bed bucking like a bronco. Then, in full view of the room's corporeal occupants, he was knocked off his feet by an invisible force.

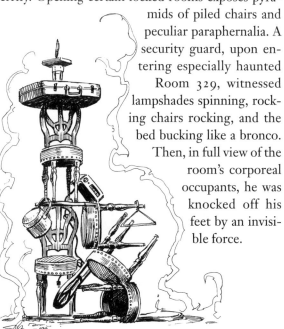

The Blind Ghost

During the early 1960s, after Manchester's "Old Schoolhouse" became the Brimlow residence, Mr. and Mrs. Brimlow were restoring the second floor. They recorded their progress in a series of photographs taken while the house was empty. In three different pictures the image of a little girl wearing a blindfold was clearly visible in the window. The ghostly child's identity remains a mystery.

Haunted Office

In the mid 1980s, owners of a newly established advertising and graphic design business on Main Street near the railroad tracks had a series of odd experiences. Various objects—pens, pencils, and rulers—vanished only to reappear elsewhere. An owner kept his prized collection of Disney mugs in a display case screwed to the wall. Somehow, it detached itself and sailed across room. A tableware drawer opened, sending airborne utensils in every direction. During renovations a worker was nailing drywall into place. Suddenly he couldn't find his hammer. Later, when for some reason he had removed the new dry wall, he found his lost hammer behind it. Yet he couldn't have installed the dry wall without the hammer. Who or what was responsible? We may never know. But perhaps the culprit was briefly glimpsed by an employee looking out a window. She saw her own reflection accompanied by that of a woman in a long dark dress standing behind her. When she turned, no one was there.

X-Rayed

The "graveyard shift" at the local hospital is occasionally enlivened by the appearance of phantoms.
One night, in the oldest part of the building, a nurse
coming out of the medical records room saw a white,
transparent human-shaped figure step out of one
wall, cross the hall, and vanish into the opposite wall.
Shaken, she made discreet inquiries and learned a
janitor had seen the apparition twice and a woman
who worked in X-ray had seen it too. All agreed it was
too late for medical intervention.

A Ghost With a Mission

In June 1982, Tony Basiliere, his new wife, and their infant son moved into a sixteen-year-old ranch house on Johnson Court. They purchased it from a widow whose husband had built it. Though it was a cheerful and comfortable place, odd things caught the couple's attention: Kitchen cabinets wouldn't stay closed; an invisible presence repeatedly reminded Tony they were not alone; the transparent form of an elderly man appeared outside the living room window. Finally, a mysterious leak in the bathroom drain suggested what the haunting was all about: When Tony opened the access panel to get at the pipes, he discovered a handgun and box of shells. The ghost vanished after that. Perhaps he'd come back to warn the young father about the secret firearm he'd left behind.

Library Caretaker

Heading north on Route 7, on the right-hand side behind the monument, is the Milton Library building. One of its two long-dead builders is still there, as if keeping an eye on it. He was most active in the tunnel that once connected it with another building. Kids in the library would often venture into places they weren't supposed to, including the tunnel. They'd get chased away by a man they thought was a security guard. They'd hear his footsteps and occasionally glimpse his tall, dark form. Only later did they learn there never had been a guard in the library or tunnel.

The Spanish Shawl

Some ghosts appear only once, do their work, and move on. For example, during the nineteenth-century a young Milton woman's most treasured possession was a beautiful Spanish shawl. Her husband hated it, saying it made her too attractive to other men. Driven by jealousy, he took her rowing on Arrowhead Lake. When he swam to shore alone, he reported their boat had capsized and she'd drowned. That night the dead woman's ghost—wearing the beautiful shawl—appeared to her sister. The ghost said, "Look for the shawl under the oak tree on the island." Next day the sister did exactly that. She found the missing woman's body and the Spanish shawl. It was soaked in blood; she had been stabbed to death. Confronted with the evidence, her husband confessed to the murder and was hanged.

Odors of the Grave?

The oddly ornate mansion on Terrace Street houses the Secretary of State and the Vermont Archives. It was built as a summer home in the 1890s by John W. Burgess. Perhaps he—or his wife Ruth—still uses it as a getaway from the spirit world. Computer equipment mysteriously fails, or works fine in one room and not another. Phones malfunction. Alarms trigger for no apparent reason. The building relights after employees have closed up for the night. Most vexing are the pleasant cooking orders that fill the building, coming perhaps from a ghostly kitchen that was long ago removed.

Grandma's Ghost?

A grandmother promised she wouldn't miss her granddaughter's wedding. Unfortunately, she died before the big day finally arrived in 1989. The wedding party assembled at the Puffer United Methodist Church on Main Street. Perhaps the bride was feeling a bit saddened by her grandmother's absence when suddenly a cool wind filled the closed church. Remarkably, it was scented with lilacs—her grandmother's favorite flower. Though no lilacs were in bloom, the fragrance was unmistakable. Was it grandma? Maybe so. Wedding photographs showed a hazy white shape right next to the bride.

Carrie's Orchard

Carrie Sumner, who earned local contempt in her time by becoming romantically involved with an Indian, just refuses to go away. For more than a century she has been spotted in the disused orchard she once owned. Sometimes she moves almost invisibly among the gnarled and twisted trees. But generally she's glimpsed standing on a ledge. She wears work boots, several layers of skirts, a tattered jacket, and a peculiar hat. In her own day Carrie was considered eccentric, but by now people are used to her.

The White Spot

In this settlement formerly known as Rich's Hollow, the Rich Mansion on Old Stage Coach Road stands like a spooky centerpiece. Built in 1805, this rare example of Georgian architecture has inspired many odd stories, including tales about treasures and ghosts. Perhaps the most unusual involves people inside the mansion who suddenly hear an odd sound. Those who have heard it say it sounds like a little dog with a "chirping bark." It is persistent, sometimes angry, so anyone trying to sleep is likely to get up to see what all the commotion is about. Some go outside to look around, but generally find nothing. But occasionally people have reported seeing a vaguely luminous white spot that travels in circles around the house. It is impossible to locate groups of corroborating witnesses though, for the "ghost dog" only manifests when someone is alone in the house.

The Stone-Throwing Devil

During October 1874, Thomas Paddock, a respectable farmer of excellent character, suddenly found his property under supernatural assault. Stones—varying in size from tiny pebbles to a twenty-pound boulder—rained down on his house and outbuildings. The stones were found to be hot, even on chill winter nights. Fearing spirits, demons, or worse, the Paddocks tried to keep the strange events a secret. But word got out and caused a sensation.

NORTH POWNAL STONES

Graveyard Shift

Over the years, in the dead of night, a number of people have seen Northfield's Phantom Gravedigger making his rounds in St. John's Roman Catholic Cemetery. Usually he's spotted with his pick and shovel, standing beside an eerily glowing lantern or walking among the headstones. Occasionally he's seen hard at work; his appearance is accompanied by the sounds of digging.

School Spirit

The Henry Prescott Chaplin Memorial Library at Norwich University has been haunted for years. People have seen books jump off the shelves, lights flip on and off, and a man in nineteenth-century garb walking around inside. Though the library was recently converted to classrooms, the ghost is apparently still there.

Good Spirits

Ghosts and spirits go hand in hand at the Norwich Inn. For years it's been haunted by "Ma" Walker, who owned it during Prohibition. She served spirits anyway. Since her 1939 death, Ma continues to serve in spirit form. The spectral innkeeper adjusts window shades, turns vacuum cleaners on and off, moves cleaning materials, then rests invisibly in rocking chairs. Occasionally she's spotted—and recognized—descending the stairs.

Ghost Academy

Odd that most Vermont police officers are trained at an academy with a ghost on staff. The former tuberculosis sanatorium is haunted by a nurse named Mary who contracted TB and died there. Those who've seen her describe a woman dressed in white. Her antics are typically ghost-like, though she once brought aspirin and water to a sick trainee. Mary is consistently perceived as friendly—a helpful, peaceful, benevolent caretaker who wants to be sure things are running smoothly.

Dawson's Creak

The old Martin Manor, part of an extinct farm that was reincarnated as Goddard College, was used for many years as a girls' dormitory. Its creepy Victorian elegance was enhanced by frequent tales of phantom footsteps in the upstairs halls. Occasionally, young women were alarmed when a transparent middle-aged man wandered into their rooms. The semivisible pacer is believed to be all that remains of a loyal butler named Dawson, who must still be dutifully making his rounds.

The Blue Ghost

In the early 1800s, mining operations along Buffalo Brook brought out the best and worst in men. One of the worst strangled an honest neighbor to steal his claim. He dumped the blue, oxygen-deprived corpse down a deserted shaft. Five years later a "blue ghost" appeared to the murderer and caused his death. Since then, the blue phantom has been seen many times in the vicinity of the abandoned mines.

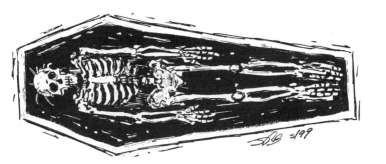

Achsa's Inspiration

Were they ghosts? Spirits? Demons? Or maybe even angels? Whatever they were, they coaxed Achsa Sprague back from near-death and sent her on a nationwide mission to upgrade the status of American women while at the same time promoting the cause of Spiritualism. Her phantom companions remained with her until 1862, when she was thirty-four years old. Then, after a prolonged illness, she joined them. The mystery of Achsa's inspiration has never been solved.

Haunted Isle

Perhaps Vermont's only truly malevolent ghost re-
sides on this sizable Lake Champlain island just west
of South Hero. There a stately summer home was
built by a wealthy family long ago. They lost their
money, legend says, and were forced to move away. In
subsequent years, many visitors to the island house
have reported the same odd events in the same
room—the one nearest the lake. During the day it
seems pleasant enough as sun streams in and water
laps the nearby shore. But at night its character
changes: Anyone sleeping there is likely to be awakened by the sounds of a man screaming into their
face, accompanied by the painful sensation of fingers
digging into their shoulders, shaking them. They'll
invariably wake up, trying to dismiss the experience
as a dream. But, fully alert, they'll be unable to shake
the sense of a male presence in the room, nor can
they quiet the ringing in their ears and tingling in
their shoulders. This terrifying scenario has played
out enough so that people suspect the ghost of a former owner may be haunting the grand house—an
owner who once tried to strangle his wife in that very
room.

No Vacancy

The Putney Inn has its roots in Vermont's colonial past. It was built around 1752 by British Captain John Kathan on acreage granted by Benning Wentworth. Today strange things happen there at night, like electric lights going on and off. But this ghost, possibly being a pre-electric sort, also relights extinguished candles in the dining room. Dina Kane, an inn employee, has witnessed the ghost's apparent objection to modern music: Every night at nine o'clock the stereo in the lounge shuts off and no one can restart it. Ms. Kane thinks she has seen the lower half of a woman walking around on the second floor. She suspects there are as many as three ghosts haunting the premises, so the inn will never be vacant.

A Tidy Spirit

Gray Gables, the grand if a bit scary-looking Boright mansion on River Street, was once used as a bed and breakfast. The owner endured a series of unexplained happenings, the most oft repeated of which was that coats and other articles of clothing carelessly abandoned would vanish, then later be discovered neatly folded and put away. A toddler's blanket disappeared from the living-room floor and was found neatly folded over the back of a dining room chair. Locals said this "tidying" behavior was consistent with that of a lady who'd once lived there. The ghost's identity became more evident when the owner tried to put a number on the bedroom that had once been hers. Try as he might, no number would stay fixed to her door.

Disturb Not the Grave

On Route 5, where the Williams River meets the Connecticut, there is a ridge above a mobile home park just north of Old River Road. It was on that scenic point that a man built a log cabin that can still be seen. Unfortunately, his modest dream house turned into a nightmare when he began work on his swimming pool. Apparently his digging disturbed a Native American or early settlers' burying ground. Formerly tranquil spirits rose up with tremendous fury and plagued him relentlessly until he abandoned the land.

Show Him the Door

Mark Massie of Colchester recalls a ghostly experience from his early adolescence. He and his brother
were playing near the family place in Ryegate. While
exploring, they found a hill with a wooden door in its
side. This wood-plank door looked ancient. So did its
rough iron bolts, oversized hinges, and huge rusty
padlock. The boys ran to tell their parents. Their
mother stopped to see the door on her way to St.
Johnsbury. She was puzzled; she'd lived there all her
life and had never seen it before. All three agreed to
explore the interior when they got back from their er-
rand. But when they returned just a few hours later,
the door was gone.

The Baby in the Cellar

In 1915, while residing in one of the twin houses on
Aldis Street, Ray and Henry Shepard were troubled
by ghosts. Ray heard footsteps descending an empty
staircase. A beckoning arm summoned Henry to the
kitchen then led him to the cellar. Later the Shepards
learned the previous occupants' baby had died in the
house and they had buried it in the cellar. The tiny
body was exhumed and the haunting stopped.

Band in St. A.

Though it has been many years since the late Martha
Collins lived in the old Collins Place on Sheldon
Road, people still hear the big band music she used to
play on her Victrola. The house has been sold several
times since her death, yet Mrs. Collins still keeps an
eye on it. Once, when the roof caught fire, a woman
answering Mrs. Collins's description rapped on the
door, pointed out the problem, and vanished.

The Kellogg House

Occupants of this well-known haunted house on Mount Pleasant Street are apt to see a stranger in their midst. People have encountered a woman in old-fashioned clothing inside the house. Sometimes the stranger walks down the stairs and into the dining room without saying a word. If followed, she'll be nowhere around. She has even been spotted outside, as if arriving. She'll walk up the front steps and into the house, but of course she can't be located within. Some speculate she is a former owner or employee—perhaps a woman named Gypsy, who lived there fifty years ago.

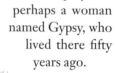

Dog Lover

St. Johnsbury Academy's Brantview House was originally a private residence. Supposedly, it's haunted by a ghost who likes dogs. A young woman employed as housemother was reading one night in the double parlor. Her Afghan hound snoozed at her feet. Suddenly the door opened. Her dog bristled and snarled at something the young woman could not see. As the animal cowered against her, she saw its fur being ruffled and smoothed as if by an invisible hand. The dog relaxed and seemed to watch something cross the parlor toward the main hall. After about twenty minutes the presence returned, shut the hall door, ruffled the dog's fur again, exited through the front parlor, and politely closed the door.

Shard Villa

This Italianate-gothic hodgepodge of Victorian ec-
centricity was built in 1872 by Columbus Smith. Following a series of family tragedies, Smith lost his
health and eventually his reason. But even death did-
n't bring rest for the energetic attorney. He's still seen
walking the halls, perhaps searching for the source of
the odd sounds that fill the ancient rooms: glass shat-
tering, a piano playing, even a baby crying.

Savage Haunts

For at least twenty years, Bill Cameron lived year round and kept a farm on Savage Island. Strange things happened there. People doing chores in the barn often reported heavy footsteps pounding in the hayloft overhead. Investigation unfailingly proved the loft to be empty. Yet something mysterious would occasionally enter the barn: First a light would be spotted soaring across the fields. Instead of stopping at the barn, it would go right through! Once Mr. Cameron and some in-laws broke for lunch while haying. They looked out over Lake Champlain and saw a small sailboat with a man, a woman, and a small boy aboard. It came right up to shore, but nobody arrived at the house. When they checked, no one was around. Though they could see for miles, there was no trace of the sailboat. The haunting—if that's what it was—was never malevolent, but could be mischievous. Sometimes, shortly after the horses were locked in the barn, they'd be spotted back out in the barnyard with their manes and tails tied in knots. Can big lakes, like the sea, play strange tricks on a man?

Invisible Sisters

Almost precisely on the boundary of Wilmington and Searsburg, the recently renovated Heather Mansion has justly acquired the reputation for being haunted. The independent and perhaps eccentric sisters Mary and Cecilia Heather built the place in 1896 and lived there for years. They may be in residence still, though their deaths were recorded long ago. Intruders during the years the place stood empty, and solitary craftsmen employed to fix it up, often reported hearing the invisible sisters chattering away in the supposedly empty rooms.

Seen by Daylight

Beginning in 1996 with a sighting by the Center Shaftsbury Cemetery caretaker, a phantom has prowled, night and day, among the gravestones. Said to resemble the character of "Doc" on Gunsmoke, the ghost is believed to be Gardner Barton, Jr., who died in 1847. Historical photographs and the phantom's propensity to hang around the Barton family tombstone aided in the identification.

Shelburne Farms

The palatial "summer house" overlooking Lake Champlain was built on 1,000 acres in 1880 by Dr. William Seward and Lila Vanderbilt Webb. Today it is still a working farm and is maintained as an inn and restaurant. But there are often more staff members and guests than expected. In the back lot, where patrons park their cars, a servant in livery is occasionally seen. Then there's the playroom on the third floor frequented by a ghostly nanny who just can't seem to stop caring. She'll turn the lights on and off or adjust the shades when all the windows are closed. Though most staff members won't talk about their resident "haunts," they are nonetheless experienced by guests at the inn.

Museum Ghost

The Dutton House was built in Cavendish, Vermont, in 1782 and moved to the Shelburne Museum in 1950, following four decades of standing vacant. The odd thing is, its ghost seems to have moved with it. The spectral occupant—perhaps its builder, Salmon

Dutton—is not an unfriendly spirit and his activities are generally benign. He seems to favor the upstairs where he flashes lights, makes noises, and occasionally, on hot summer days, somehow causes a cold wind to blow through the rooms. When he rests he does so in a particular bed, for it is often found disturbed in the morning. Over the years many museum employees and volunteers have preferred not to work in the building alone—though it can be argued that no one is ever alone in the Dutton house.

Library Prankster

The ghost at the Pierson Library on the Green in Shelburne has for years played pranks on staff and volunteers. He'll move heavy bags of books the full length of a six-foot work table or shove heavy boxes across the floor. And he's not shy; he does it in full view of anyone in the room. Long-time assistant librarian Brenda Withey says he once arranged all the books in a locked storage cupboard to form a serpentine staircase. But the prankster can also be helpful. Once, when Brenda remarked that a storm might be coming, heavy windows moved up, against gravity, then closed, and locked all by themselves. Brenda watched in disbelief.

Midnight Cow

Along Route 74, between the towns of Shoreham and Cornwall, is property that once belonged to the old Farrington Farm. The once prosperous dairy operation failed in the early 1960s after a string of almost preternaturally bad luck. The catalyst for the rapid-fire misfortune occurred in 1952 when one of Farrington's prize Holsteins escaped the pasture through a broken fence. It wandered on to the macadam, where it was struck by a bread truck. Though Mr. Farrington and his wife are long gone, the cow is still occasionally spotted on that stretch of road. Only its white markings and red glowing eyes are visible in the darkness. More than one frightened driver has collided with the apparition, only to discover he has hit nothing at all.

Emily's Bridge

Vermont's only haunted covered bridge hosts the phantom of a teenage girl who killed herself after a lovers' quarrel. Seemingly, she still waits for her boyfriend to return, getting angrier by the year. Emily's ghost is accused of slashing livestock and scratching automobile paint jobs. She's been heard, felt, and photographed. And—as Vermont's most famous spook—has earned a reputation that extends far beyond the natural boundaries of her native state.

Nothing's Fishy

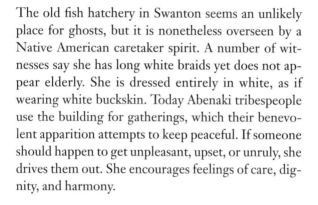

The old fish hatchery in Swanton seems an unlikely place for ghosts, but it is nonetheless overseen by a Native American caretaker spirit. A number of witnesses say she has long white braids yet does not appear elderly. She is dressed entirely in white, as if wearing white buckskin. Today Abenaki tribespeople use the building for gatherings, which their benevolent apparition attempts to keep peaceful. If someone should happen to get unpleasant, upset, or unruly, she drives them out. She encourages feelings of care, dignity, and harmony.

What Are You Doing Here?

The octagonal Lightgate Learning Center off Houghton Hill is rumored to be built on Indian land and is said to be cursed. Strange things happen there, though few seem attributable to malediction: People practice alternative healing or study intuitive science and spiritual growth. "Max" the Crystal Skull puts in occasional guest appearances. But something far more baffling appeared to Prof. Leonard Gibson— perhaps a visitor from another realm. While spending the night, he was awakened by an aggressive tugging on his bedcovers. An opaque, long-haired, apparently female apparition that appeared to be edged by light confronted him and seemed to demand, "What are you doing here? What are you doing here?" Shaken by the startling vision, Dr. Gibson may well have asked it the same question.

The Photo Phantom

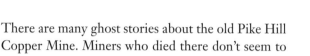

There are many ghost stories about the old Pike Hill Copper Mine. Miners who died there don't seem to go away. And those who died elsewhere seem to come back. A Ryegate family has proof of these spectral visitors. On a weekend outing they visited the abandoned mine where the wife's father had worked for many years. Her husband took a picture of her standing in front of a large rock. The surprise came when the film was developed. There, big as life, as if standing *within* the rock, was the woman's father. No question, he was with her in the photograph, though he had been dead for many years.

Green Mountain Seminary

The three-and-a-half-story, rust-colored Green Mountain Seminary on Route 100 was used as a school until 1969. Supposedly, an art teacher who drew up on the top floor died there. But maybe he still walks the halls. Around 1980, something scared a bunch of men from the building. Their basketball game was interrupted by pounding overhead. They searched for its source, but when they couldn't find it they became frightened and fled. Some vowed never to return.

The Trembling House

International ghost hunter James Reynolds tells of an odd haunting he discovered while driving from Waterford to St. Johnsbury. An abandoned house nearly concealed by maple trees seemed to actually shake on its brick foundation—but in utter silence. Beside it, the ghostly form of a woman stared, with an expression of profound hatred. The woman, he was sure, was a ghost. The house may be spectral as well.

Ghost Hollow

Perhaps the only part of Vermont named after a ghost. Prior to rail travel, a young man was hurrying home on Lake Champlain to be with his wife for the arrival of their first-born. Rushing from the wharf toward his log cabin, he encountered his wife in the woods. Her radiant image suddenly vanished and he knew the truth. When he reached home, she was dead. Since then, the spot appears on maps as "Ghost Hollow."

Whipple Hollow

About three miles north of West Rutland sits the abandoned town of Whipple Hollow. Little visible evidence remains of its heyday in the marble industry . . . but something ghostly lingers. It is an especially haunted and mysterious area. There's a spot by a pond where voices call out at midnight. A profound and unnatural darkness occasionally descends, so dense car headlights won't penetrate it. Frank Kurant recalls meeting the beautiful phantom of Whipple Hollow Road. He stopped to offer her a ride one snowy night, but when he reached to open the passenger door, she vanished. Only her footprints remained, ending abruptly in the undisturbed snow.

Fanny's Phantoms

Fanny was the youngest of Ethan Allen's three children. Like her father, she scorned organized religion. After Ethan's death, Fanny's mother married Dr. Jabez Penniman and moved to Westminster, Vermont. There, on the shore of the Connecticut River, Fanny had an extraordinary experience. While walking along one clear day, she saw something ominous and evil emerging from the water. She described it as being "of extraordinary size and horrid shape." Though she wanted to run from the nightmarish apparition, she was unable to move. Certain the looming creature meant her great harm, she attempted to cry for help, but could not. "While I was in this torturing situation," she said, "I saw advancing towards me a man of venerable and striking countenance, wearing a brown cloak and carrying a staff in his hand. He took me gently by the arm and gave me strength to move while he said most kindly to me: 'My child, what are you doing here? Hasten away.' I then ran as fast as I could." Fanny later became convinced her rescuer was St. Joseph. This conviction led her to the Catholic Church and her life as a healer. The demonic shape that rose from the Connecticut River was never identified. Could it still be there?

A Premature Ghost

In 1919, Frank Nugelo and two other men were berry picking on the grounds of the deserted Nearney farm in Weston. The men knew the house had been empty for a long time, so they were surprised when they saw a figure in the window looking out at them. The figure was robed and seemed to have a hood over his head. It looked like a priest or monk. When the men went to investigate, the house was empty and there were no tracks in the heavy dust on the floor. Decades later the building was purchased by monks, who turned it into the Weston Priory.

White House, Brown Ghost

The White House Inn, a magnificent turn-of-the-century mansion, was built by lumber baron Martin Brown and his wife Clara. One can see why they hated to leave—even after death. Today it is maintained as a beautiful inn, and the late Clara Brown still walks the halls. Noises, creaks, cold spots, and even a face-to-face confrontation show that she is still around. Occasionally the spirit even speaks to someone—but only if their name happens to also be Brown.

3/99

Watermans' Water Sprite

In 1955 the Cherry Street home of Dr. Thomas Waterman began to flood. Trouble is, no one could determine the source of the water. It just seemed to appear. In the first two days the family cleaned up thirteen buckets full. Later, it even rained inside the house. Eventually the demented deluge drove the family from their home. Then, a month later, things returned to normal, leaving water damage and an impossible mystery.

The Phantom Walker

The Winooski railroad trestle, known locally as "The Blue Bridge," is supposedly the scene of a suicide by hanging. Is it his phantom, or someone else's, that's occasionally spotted there? People walking the tracks will see another pedestrian coming toward them, crossing the trestle. But as they get closer, the figure on the bridge vanishes.

Haunted High School

In 1960, seven students were killed in an automobile accident. Their funeral was held in the high school gym. Since that day, events suggest they haven't moved on to higher education. Invisible feet pound on empty bleachers. A water bucket rose in the air and spilled. Janitor Jim Lefebvre heard loud footsteps in empty rooms and a disembodied voice calling his name. Others witnessed ghostly apparitions moving in the halls at night when the school was locked and supposedly vacant.

The Phantom Highwayman

A century ago a "plank road" or "log turnpike" was built through Snail Swamp, stretching from Woodstock to Windsor. Years later a solitary rider, dressed entirely in black, was spotted from time to time, splashing along the rotted timbers, intent on business no living soul could fathom. Who he is—or was—is a mystery, as is why he patrols Snail Swamp. Apparently he always travels toward Woodstock. And apparently he never gets where he is going.

Acknowledgments

The stories in this book come from diverse sources. Some were culled from my earlier work: *Green Mountains, Dark Tales*; *Passing Strange*; *Green Mountain Ghosts*; and the commentary series I have been doing on Vermont Public Radio since 1991.

Many individuals helped me to pull new stories together, and I have used numerous printed resources. In earlier volumes I cited my sources and thanked individual contributors.

But some people aided specifically with this volume and made contributions unique to *The Vermont Ghost Guide*.

I especially want to acknowledge Mariella Squire, who was more than generous with the fascinating ghostlore she has collected over the years.

I also want to thank Bernice Kelman along with Annie and Louis DiSpirito for a wonderful afternoon of swapping ghost stories—most of which they had actually experienced.

Each of the following people was kind enough to contribute a story, a lead, a bit of vital information, or some much-needed moral support. I want to thank each of these honorary ghostbusters. They are: Dana Basiliere, Tony Basiliere, Jane Beck, Anna Blackmer, Marge Bleier, Tim Brooks, Genevieve Burke, Flora Chicoine, David Cole, Jim DeFilippi, Sandy Duffina, Travis Fahey, Diane E. Foulds, Gary Frazier, Jen Freedman, Jennifer Fries, Leonard and Elizabeth Gibson, Annette Goyne, Lou and Gwen Hill, Gail Hudson, Denise Johnson, Dina Kane, Frank Kurant, Michael Lavery, Garet Livermore, Sue McEvoy, Mark

Massie, Marion Nugelo, Gary Olivetti, Peter Patten, Pamela Polston, Greg Sharrow, Gary Snider, Matthew Sturridge, Janice Szabo, Michael Taft, Rick Veitch, Tim and Sally Wilson, and Brenda Withey. My sincerest apologies to any who, because of their request or my failing memory, I have left out.

About the Creators

Both native Vermonters, Stephen R. Bissette and Joseph A. Citro have worked together, as illustrator and writer, on the first edition of Mr. Citro's novel *Deus-X* and the *Vermont's Haunts Map*, as well as *The Vermont Ghost Guide*.

Stephen R. Bissette worked in the comic book industry for over two decades as an artist and co-plotter for DC Comics' *Saga of the Swamp Thing* (1983–87), editor/publisher of the anthology *Taboo* (1988–95), and writer/artist/self-publisher of *S. R. Bissette's Tyrant* (1994–97), and more. He has illustrated a book a year since 1989 — including this one—while writing for many film magazines and books. He most recently co-authored *The Monster Book: Buffy the Vampire Slayer* (2001), authored and self-published *We Are Going to Eat You: The Third World Cannibal Films* (2003), and is completing a book on Vermont films and filmmakers.

Joe Citro, novelist and storyteller, is well known as a collector of offbeat Vermontiana. He has chronicled the oddities of local history on public radio, in his popular lectures, and in a series of best-selling books including *Green Mountains, Dark Tales, Passing Strange,* and *Green Mountain Ghosts*. Additionally, Mr. Citro is the author of five acclaimed Vermont-based novels: *Shadow Child, Guardian Angels, The Gore, Lake Monsters,* and *Deus-X: The Reality Conspiracy*.

Author and oddity collector

Joe Citro

would like to hear your stories
of Vermont's odd, unusual,
and just plain weird.
You can write to him in care of

UNIVERSITY PRESS OF NEW ENGLAND

ONE COURT STREET

LEBANON, NH 03766

Or you can contact him via email at:
stories@burlcol.edu
www.JosephACitro.com

Library of Congress Cataloging-in-Publication Data
Citro, Joseph A.

    The Vermont ghost guide / stories by Joseph A. Citro ;
art by Stephen R. Bissette.

       p.   cm.

    ISBN 1–58465–009–5 (pbk.: alk. paper)

    1. Ghosts—Vermont. 2. Haunted places—Vermont. I.
Title.

BF1472.U6 C53 2000

133.1'09743—dc21   99–55973